CONTEMPORARY'S
Reading
Basics

Intermediate 1 Reader

Mc Graw Hill **Wright Group**

 **Wright Group**

ISBN: 0-8092-0667-6

Send all inquiries to:
Wright Group/McGraw-Hill
130 E. Randolph, Suite 400
Chicago, IL 60601
Manufactured in the United States of America.

8 9 10 CUS CUS 08 07 06

The *McGraw·Hill* Companies

Table of Contents

To the Reader

If reading has never been easy for you, Contemporary's *Reading Basics* will help. Each selection in this reader will let you practice reading. The article or story will grab your interest and keep you reading to the end. When you finish reading, you will answer questions to

- check your understanding of the story
- apply reading skills to help your understanding of the story

You may answer these questions alone or with your classmates. You might write the answers or you might use the questions to have a discussion. Suggested answers to the questions are in the back of this book.

Your teacher may ask you to read a selection after a lesson in the workbook that ends with a Read On note. Or you may read these selections any time you wish.

Reading Basics will build your confidence in your ability to read by letting you practice on short, interesting stories.

Long Live Verdi!

Who was Giuseppe Verdi? Why do people still listen to his music?

1 Verdi's music is everywhere. It is heard on stage, in films, and in TV programs. Every day of the year, at least one of Verdi's operas is performed live somewhere in the world.

A Poor Son of Italy

2 Giuseppe Verdi [jyoo•zep'•pee vair'•dee] was born in Italy in 1813. His parents were poor, so Verdi had little schooling. But even as a young boy, he showed a talent for music. People in his hometown knew that Verdi was gifted. On his own, he learned to play the organ. Soon he was the best organist in town.

3 Antonio Barezzi [bah•reh'•tzee] lived in the same town as Verdi. He liked music and offered to help the young man. Barezzi paid for the 18-year-old Verdi's studies in the city of Milan. After three years, Verdi came back to his hometown. He took the job of music director. In 1836, Verdi married Barezzi's daughter.

Time of Sadness

4 Verdi wanted a bigger job. He wanted to write operas. He could not do that in a small town. So he went back to Milan. There he wrote *Oberto*. It was not a great opera, but it was good enough to be staged. The head of a theater asked Verdi to write three more works.

5 Then came tragedy. Verdi's wife and two small children became ill and died. Verdi struggled through his grief to write a second opera. But *King for a Day* was a total flop. The audience booed. Verdi was a broken man. He vowed never to write music again.

Success

6 Verdi kept his word for more than a year. Then the head of the theater showed him a new story. He asked Verdi to put it to music. Verdi said no but agreed to read the story. It was a Bible tale about Hebrew slaves. Verdi was deeply moved by the story. He began to set its words to music. Verdi called his new opera *Nabucco* [nah•boo'•koh]. Staged in 1842, *Nabucco* took Italy by storm. The opera was a triumph. Verdi became famous in Italy.

7 Verdi was back on track. For the next few years, he wrote day and night. In the 1840s, he wrote more than one opera a year. That is a lot of music to write in so short a time. Most composers need about two or three years to write just one opera. Verdi wrote quickly but well. He was Italy's best composer. And his finest works were still to come.

More Great Music

8 In 1851, Verdi wrote the opera *Rigoletto.* It was a great success. (A TV ad uses a song from this work to sell doughnuts.) Verdi then wrote *Il Trovatore* [el troh•vah•toh'•ray]. This opera and his next, *La Traviata* [la trah•vyah'•tah], were also smash hits. (A song from *La Traviata* can be heard in a soft drink ad on TV.)

9 These last three works made Verdi world famous. People like his operas for many reasons. The songs are simple but tuneful. They are as easy to recall as today's pop tunes. Verdi's songs, with their lively rhythms, stir people's feelings.

10 Like Broadway musicals, Verdi's operas are great shows. Each one is a feast for the eye, the ear, and the heart. The singers wear fine costumes, and the sets on stage are beautiful.

11 Verdi chose exciting stories. The people in them have real-life problems and strong feelings. In this way, the opera plots are like those of good movies or books. In opera, though, the actors pour out their feelings in song. They sing of love, hope, fear, hate, murder, and revenge. They even sing about having fun. The strong feelings in Verdi's music give the drama much more power than words alone could. The music can make the listener laugh in one scene and cry in the next.

Branching Out

12 Verdi's fame grew. He was a superstar. Heads of other nations asked him to write music for special events. Verdi wrote some works for the Paris

Opera, in France. His opera called *The Force of Destiny* was first produced in Russia. Verdi then wrote *Aida* [ah•ee'•dah] for the opening of the Suez Canal in Egypt.

Two More Operas

13   By 1871, Verdi had written 26 operas. He thought that he had done enough. He planned to retire. He went to live on his farm near his hometown. His friend Boito [boh•ee'•toh] paid Verdi a visit. Boito had written the words for a new tragic opera. It was based on a play by William Shakespeare. Boito's words needed music. Verdi could not resist the call to write a new opera. At the age of 74, he wrote *Otello.* Some people say it is his greatest work.

14   Verdi again planned to stop writing music. But Boito wrote the words for one more opera. As with *Otello,* the new story was based on a Shakespeare play. This time, though, the story was a comedy. Verdi was 80 years old when he wrote *Falstaff.* He wrote the opera for fun. He did not care if it was ever performed on stage. *Falstaff* was indeed performed. It was, to no one's surprise, another winner.

Lasting Gifts

15   At last, Verdi retired from writing operas. Still, he wrote some fine church music. Verdi's health began to fail. In 1901, he suffered a stroke and died.

16   Verdi wanted to give old musicians a place to live when they retired. Years before he died, Verdi

set up a retirement home in Milan. It is called Casa Verdi, which means "Verdi Home." The composer left most of his money to Casa Verdi. The home is still in use today.

17   "Long Live Verdi!" was the cry in Verdi's time. It praised a man of Italy who gave the world so much great music. Verdi *did* live a long time. But his music will live longer. You might not get to the opera. But you might hear a Verdi song the next time you turn on the TV. Perhaps that short ad will make you want to hear the tune the way Verdi first wrote it.

Questions

1. What role did Barezzi play in Verdi's life?
2. Why did Verdi almost give up music as a young man?
3. Which opera was Verdi's first big hit?
4. Why was it so hard for Verdi to retire?
5. Why are Verdi's operas still popular?

Antonym/Synonym Search

1. How many synonyms can you think of for each of the following words: *liked, offered, ill, famous, quickly, beautiful?*

2. Choose a paragraph in "Long Live Verdi!" and rewrite it, substituting synonyms for as many words as you can.

3. Think of antonyms for the following words: *poor, young, daughter, bigger, good, success, short, best.*

4. Use a pair of antonyms in a sentence that tells how Verdi's music is different from another kind of music that you like.

Dogs Who "Think"

Police dogs and guide dogs for the blind are working dogs. Why are they most often German shepherds?

1 The saying "Dogs are people's best friends" is an old one. People and dogs have lived together since ancient times. Many dogs serve only as pets. But some dogs have real jobs to do. They work as police dogs and as guide dogs for the blind.

2 Some breeds of dog do these jobs better than others. Very often, people choose German shepherds for this work. What makes these dogs so good at it?

The Right Stuff

3 For one thing, German shepherds are the right size. They are quite large, and they are strong. With big chests, they can get enough wind for long runs. But their chests are not too big. So their steps stay steady when they walk and run. A thick coat of fur protects them in bad weather. It also helps the dogs stay clean.

4   They look alert and are very smart. So it is easy to train them to do hard jobs. What's more, German shepherds have the right traits. Most dogs tend to be loyal, good friends. But these dogs will do what it takes to please their owners. They are willing animals. They are patient and can wait quietly for a long time. The dogs' calm and gentle natures show they can be well trained.

Poor Choices

5 Why do other dogs not work out as well? A dachshund [dahks'•hoont] is not large enough for such jobs. And a dachshund does not have the right nature. These dogs are smart enough for training. But they like to avoid doing things they don't want to do.

6   Another poor choice is a poodle. A poodle may be smarter than a German shepherd. It can train much faster than a shepherd dog. But poodles don't have good judgment. If a poodle led a blind person, it would do everything the person said. When that person said "Forward," the poodle would go forward, even if a car was coming! On the other hand, a German shepherd is not only glad to help people. This dog also knows when *not* to follow an order!

7   A German shepherd also has a lot of heart—the dog wants to be of help. Though tired or even hurt, a German shepherd will keep going.

Training

8 Trainers work a long time to prepare the dogs for their work. They choose the dogs when they are

still puppies. Police dogs train in a police barracks. But future guide dogs start their training another way. They live with a family for a year. In a home, they get used to being around all kinds of people.

9   When training starts, a police dog learns how to attack, but only does so on command. First the dog bites a rag that the trainer waves in front of his own face. Then the dog practices on a person who wears thick arm pads. The dog learns to attack and hold onto someone. But the dog does not bite that person. Most of the time, police dogs don't have to attack. When people see police dogs coming, they give up. This is true even in prison fights.

10   Police dogs also learn to search for things. To teach this skill, a trainer first throws a stick for the dog to fetch. All dogs like to go after sticks. But a police dog learns to fetch other things too.

11   Next, the trainer lets the dog sniff an object. In this way, the dog learns the smell of the thing it is going to look for. Then the trainer hides the object far away. The dog must not see the trainer hide it. The dog then searches the area part by part. The dog's careful plan and keen sense of smell leave no spot unchecked. A dog can find almost anything by its smell.

On the Job

12 A trained German shepherd can find something even when it doesn't know what the object is. The trainer just says "Search," and the dog is on its way. It shows the trainer anything that seems out of place. Maybe a bank robber buried some loot. The dog finds any newly dug patches of dirt. Or, the

robber might be hiding. The dog walks right past other people and finds the one police want. If the dog is looking for a missing person, it starts at that person's home. Of all the foot tracks in the house, the dog must sniff out the freshest set.

Guide Dogs

13   Like a police dog, a guide dog needs a lot of training. A guide dog must also use good judgment. The dog's "work clothes" for this job are a guide harness. In the harness, the dog learns to walk to the left and just ahead of the trainer. Outdoors the dog must learn to steer clear of trees and people. It must also learn to give its owner room to avoid these things, too.

14   A guide dog must guess ahead of time how high and wide things are. For example, an owner might be headed for a low tree branch. A well-trained dog can tell that the branch is too low in time to lead the owner around it.

15   The dog must know why it is being trained. Knowing this helps the dog act wisely when faced with a new problem. For example, a guide dog learns to stop at each curb when crossing a street. But just stopping is not enough if that stop also leads the owner into a ditch nearby. The dog must understand that the goal of training is to keep the owner safe. Then the dog makes the choices that protect the owner.

A Working Team

16   Training centers match guide dogs with blind persons. Just one blind person in ten can learn to

use a guide dog. The person has to like dogs. He or she should also be willing to learn new ways to do everyday things. The dog and the new owner train together for about a month. Then the owner takes the dog to its new home. They will both start a new life as a working team.

17   It may be a pet, a police dog, or a guide dog. In many ways, a German shepherd shows it is indeed a person's best friend.

Questions

1. Give two reasons why German shepherds make good police dogs and guide dogs.

2. Name two breeds of dog that are poor choices for police and guide dogs.

3. How is the start of training for a guide dog different from that for a police dog?

4. Describe two different jobs that a police dog may be given.

5. Out of every ten blind persons, about how many can learn to use a guide dog?

Using Context Clues

Before answering these questions, first find the underlined word or phrase in the selection and determine its meaning from context clues in that passage.

1. What are you least likely to do in a barracks: sing, sleep, ski, or have supper?

2. Why must guide dogs have good judgment?

3. What does it mean to attack on command?

Dark Days

Would you like to live in a land with dark days and "white nights"?

1 Days are light. Nights are dark. That's how most of the world thinks of day and night. But the people of Iceland and parts of Norway, Sweden, and Finland don't think that way. To them, winter days are as dark as night.

2 The sun is what makes daylight. When the sun drops below the horizon of any place on Earth, the sky becomes dark. To most people in the world, that means night. But in winter, in northern Scandinavia [Skan•dih•nay'•vee•ah], the sun never makes it above the horizon at all. So, there is no daylight. Days are dark, just like nights.

The Arctic Circle

3 Scandinavia is really five countries: Denmark, Finland, Iceland, Norway, and Sweden. Iceland and parts of Norway, Sweden, and Finland fall within the Arctic [Ark'•tik] Circle. In those northern places, days are dark for six weeks. There

is also a great deal of snow and ice to deal with—
and to enjoy.

4   Cold, dark winters have always played a big
part in the lives of Scandinavian people. This is
seen in many of the folktales of the land. The trolls
of the old stories hated sun, but the people loved it.
The frost giants of other tales stood for the force of
the harsh winters. They fought against all that was
good. In story after story, the faraway light of
summer stood for hope.

Autumn-Winter

5 In the northern parts of Scandinavia, there are three
winters: autumn-winter, high-winter, and spring-
winter. Autumn-winter is in October and
November, the elk-hunting season. Some say this
first winter is the worst. The beautiful snow has not
yet come. There is still some daylight. Yet everyone
knows the darkness is on its way.

High-Winter Fun

6 The last day with any light at all is in December.
This is the beginning of high-winter. The snow and
ice come, but they are beautiful in the dark. The
moon and stars seem brighter against the snow.
This is also the time of the northern lights. Bits of
the sun break off and pass through the sky as red,
blue, and white arcs of light.

7   During high-winter, many northern
Scandinavians go south, like the birds. But those
who stay home in the dark can have plenty of fun.
This is the time when friends get together most

often. There are plays and music to enjoy. And there are the many winter sports for which the Scandinavian countries are famous.

8   Children learning to walk learn to ski at the same time. Three or more feet of snow cover the ground every day. People cross-country ski to get where they want to go. Children may go to school in the dark and come home in the dark. But they also have days off to go skiing. Ice skating is a favorite winter activity. Ice-hole fishing keeps many people busy. Iceboating and ice hockey are popular sports.

Special Problems

9   But the winter is not all fun and games. There are a great number of winter problems to deal with. For many people, the "winter blues" come with the darkness. Many people have trouble sleeping, even though it is dark. Everyone has to dress in warm, heavy clothes and boots just to go outside. Everyone wears a fur hat.

10   The cost of heat is high. To keep the heat in and save money, windows have three layers of glass. Some windows are made with metal-plated glass to bounce indoor heat back into the home. To keep out the cold, walls are very thick. Some doors are so heavy they are hard to open. Nearly every home has a fireplace or stove with a damper to keep out cold air.

A Way of Life

11   Northern Scandinavians make up for the darkness by making their own light. Though the sky is dark,

all kinds of bright lights flood the towns. If you flew over Scandinavia during the winter, you would see many, many lights. The number of lights is high for the number of people living in this land.

12   While all of this may seem odd, the northern people are used to their dark winters. "The sun is a strange object in the sky that you rarely see in winter," says one woman from Finland. "I don't think much about the darkness. It seems normal." Some people in this land even say a baby born in the winter is two nights old, rather than two days old.

13   On January 21, the sun rises high enough to give four minutes of daylight. The people of northern Scandinavia have parties to welcome the light.

Spring-Winter

14 March and April mark spring-winter, the third winter season. Little by little, the days grow longer. But the snow and ice melt into brown slush. Roads are covered with mud. Spring-winter is not a pretty time. The long winter finally gives way to the short, beautiful summer. The weather is warm but not hot. This is called the time of flowers. By July, the northern days are so long that there is no darkness at all. These are the "white nights." That's why the Arctic Circle is called the "land of the midnight sun."

15   To the people of northern Scandinavia, summer is very special. They get out and enjoy it. Or they go on holiday for months at a time. They know that soon enough the dark days of winter will be upon them once again.

Questions

1. Which countries make up Scandinavia?

2. Name the three kinds of winter in the Arctic Circle.

3. How do the people of this land make up for the darkness during winter?

4. Why is the Artic Circle called "the land of the midnight sun"?

5. Which sport would you expect to be more popular in Scandinavia, sailing or basketball? Why?

Spelling Word Alert

1. Find the sentences that use the following words: *sun, great, there, so, seen, break, four*. Write a homophone for each of those words.

2. Add the suffix *-ness* to a word in the title. Find from two to four sentences in the selection that use this word.

3. Find the sentences with the words *enjoy* and *thick*. Add a suffix to each word, and write a sentence using each new word.

Diamonds: Stars from Earth

Why do diamonds hold such power over people?

1 Diamonds have many names. The ancient Greeks used to call them "stars fallen from Earth." Other people said they were "God's tears." A song once called them "a girl's best friend."

2 Diamonds are best known as a symbol of romance. The Greeks thought that the "fire" in a diamond was like the fire of love. In 1477, an Austrian duke gave the first diamond engagement ring to his future bride. Jewelers around the world should thank that duke!

3 Women wear an engagement ring on the third finger of the left hand. This custom, too, goes back a long way. The ancient Egyptians thought that the "vein of love" ran to that finger. They thought it ran straight from the heart.

4 What makes diamonds so popular? In truth, they are simple stones. Diamonds are pure carbon.

In a way, they are like the graphite [graf'•ite] in a lead pencil. But turning carbon into a diamond is not a simple task. Deep in the Earth, great heat and pressure change the carbon. And diamonds need much time to form. It takes about three billion years to make a diamond.

The Making of a Diamond

5   No one knows for sure how diamonds were created. Most likely they formed in molten rock far below the earth's crust.

6   At some time long ago, this rock was pushed upward. It broke through the earth's crust and cooled in funnel-shaped "pipes." Most diamonds are mined from such pipes.

7   Mining diamonds is harder than it may sound. To find one good stone, miners must dig through about 250 tons of ore. In all of history, miners have dug up only about 350 tons of diamonds.

Beautiful Yet Strong

8   Diamonds are popular stones for rings and earrings. They may also gleam in the crown of a king or queen.

9   But diamonds also have a practical side. They are the hardest substance found on Earth. So they make great drill points. Diamonds that are not good enough to be gem stones are used in this way. Most diamonds, in fact, find their way to the tip of a drill.

The Four C's

10   People who sell diamond gems judge them by the four C's. The C's are cut, color, clarity, and carat weight. The value of a diamond depends on all four C's.

11   A diamond begins as a rough stone. But it can have many shapes. A diamond may be round or oval. It may be shaped like a pear or a heart. A diamond cutter looks at the shape. Then he or she cuts the stone so it will reflect light and sparkle brightly.

12   Diamonds come in many colors. They can be a very pale yellow or brown. Some rare gems are blue, pink, or green. The rarest color of all is red. Many people say that *no* color is best. A colorless diamond turns white light into a rainbow of colors.

13   Clarity is another word for clearness. Most diamonds have tiny flaws. Some are in the stone itself, but others are on the surface. These flaws may show up when light passes through the stone. Good clarity adds to a stone's value. A flawless diamond is very rare.

14   Last, there is the stone's size. Diamonds are weighed in carats. There are about 142 carats in one ounce. Size, however, isn't everything. Two diamonds of the same weight may not have the same value. The other three C's help decide the value.

Famous Diamonds

15   One of the most famous diamonds is the Koh-i-Noor [koh'•uh•nur]. The name means

"mountain of light." This gem once weighed 186 carats. It was recut for the queen of England. Now the diamond weights 108 carats. It is part of the British crown jewels.

16   Even bigger was the Cullinan [kul'•ih•nun] diamond. It was the largest diamond ever found. As a rough stone, it weighed over 3000 carats. Then it was cut into 9 large stones and 96 small ones. One of these large gems is the famed Star of Africa. It weighs 530 carats. That makes it the world's largest cut diamond.

17   But perhaps the most famous gem of all is the Hope diamond. The diamond has a curse on it, the legend says. Everyone who has owned it has had bad luck.

18   The "curse" has struck again and again. Marie Antoinette [an•twuh•net'], the queen of France, once owned the stone. She later had her head chopped off. Lord Francis Hope once owned it. He died without a penny. A prince gave the stone to a girlfriend. He later shot her dead after a lover's quarrel. Other owners also suffered misery.

19   No one has to worry about the curse anymore. The Hope diamond is now safe. It is on display behind glass. You can see it at the Smithsonian Institution, a museum in Washington, D.C.

Questions

1. Name an ancient belief about diamonds.

2. Why are diamonds so rare?

3. What are the two uses for diamonds?

4. Why is the Hope diamond so famous?

Recalling Details

1. What are diamonds made of?

2. What are the four C's?

3. What is the rarest color of diamond?

4. How many carats are there in one ounce?

The Courage of Harry Wu

Why do Chinese communists hate Harry Wu?

1 Some people have strong beliefs. They think that all people should be free. A few people are willing to risk their lives for their beliefs. One of these people is Harry Wu, who will not give up his fight for human rights.

2 In China, government officials hate Harry Wu. To them, he is a troublemaker. In the United States, though, government officials praise him. To them, Wu is a brave man.

3 Who is Harry Wu? Why does he inspire both hate and praise?

Forced Labor

4 Harry Wu was born in China in 1937. His family was rich. He went to the best schools. His future

looked bright. Then, when he was 12, communists took over the country.

5   Wu learned to hate communists. They gave people little freedom. They also tried to impose their system on other countries. Wu spoke out against them. Of course, he got in trouble. In 1960, Wu was arrested. The communists sent him to a prison camp. It was a forced-labor camp. Prisoners were forced to work long, hard hours.

6   Wu spent the next 19 years in prison camps. He almost starved to death. So he learned to catch snakes and skin them with his teeth. He also dug up rat burrows to find bits of grain to eat.

7   In the prison camps, Wu saw many of his friends die. Some of them starved to death. Others were shot. Somehow, though, Wu survived.

A Fresh Start

8   At last, in 1979, the communists freed Wu. He got a job as a geology teacher. In 1985, Wu came to the United States to study. He had just $40 in his pocket. He slept on park benches until he found work in a doughnut shop. He worked, studied, and slowly made a good life for himself.

9   But Wu could not forget the past. Sometimes he cried when he thought about his friends in the camps. Wu felt a sense of duty to them. He had to do something to help them. So he wrote about the forced-labor camps.

10   Harry Wu's words shocked people. He wrote about torture in the camps. He wrote about forced labor. He told about the goods made in the labor

camps. These goods were being sold in the United States. It is against the law to buy such goods.

11   Wu also wrote about murder in the camps. Prisoners were sometimes shot for their body organs. Then doctors used the organs for transplants.

A Dangerous Choice

12 Wu knew he was writing the truth. But other people had some doubts. Were the communists really that bad?

13   To prove the truth, Wu chose to go back to China. It was a dangerous thing to do. In the United States, he was safe. He had a wife and a good job. He could have stayed where he was and gone on with his life. But Wu had a mission. He wanted real proof of what went on in the camps. And he was willing to risk his life to get it.

14   Harry Wu went back to China. He had false papers that said he was someone else. He also changed his looks and wore clothing that hid who he really was. Then, using a hidden camera, he filmed the forced-labor camps. He talked to doctors, hospital workers, and patients. He talked to prisoners in the camps. The camps were as bad as he remembered. Three times, he went safely into and out of China. Each time, he brought back photos and videotapes to show the world.

Back to Prison

15 During his fourth trip to China, though, Wu did not get out. In 1995, he was caught by border

guards in China. He spent the next 66 days in
prison. He was held in a tiny cell. Prison guards
questioned him day and night. Wu was sure he
would be killed. "I had to prepare for my death,"
he said.

16   One important thing saved him. Years before,
Harry Wu had become an American citizen. What's
more, the governments of the United States,
Europe, and Australia pressed China to free him.
The communists did not dare kill Harry Wu. Too
many people knew and cared about him.

Trial and Freedom

17 The communists were hard on Wu. He lost weight.
He was not allowed to shave or get enough sleep.
At last, Wu was forced to "confess" to a false
charge. His wife, Ching-lee Wu, called the
confession "a joke."

18   Meanwhile, the rest of the world was in an
uproar. People held rallies in Hong Kong, London,
and Los Angeles to "Free Harry Wu."

19   The world view of Wu's treatment put pressure
on China. The officials there had to punish Wu.
But they feared that world reports of such abuse
could turn countries against China. Then no one
would want to do business there.

20   In the end, the officials put Wu on trial. They
held the trial behind close doors. The court found
Wu guilty of spying and kicked him out of China.
Within a few hours, Wu was on a plane headed
home.

The Fight Goes On

21 Harry Wu risked his life for others. But he did not give up his fight. He would do anything to tell the world about the abuses in China.

22 So Harry Wu goes on speaking against the horrors of the camps. He says he has no choice. Human rights and freedom are too important to him.

Questions

1. Why was Harry Wu arrested in 1960?
2. What were the forced-labor camps like?
3. Why did Wu go back to China?
4. What happened to Wu in 1995 during his 66 days as a prisoner?
5. Why didn't the communists kill Wu after his 1995 arrest?

Identifying Sequence

1. Did Harry Wu become an American citizen before or after he made his fourth trip back to China?

2. Number these events in the order in which they happened.

   _____   Harry Wu wrote about the prison camps.

   _____   Harry Wu was convicted of spying.

   _____   Harry Wu got a job as a geology teacher.

The Great Seal of the United States

Why did Americans choose the eagle as a national symbol?

1 Back in 1776, Americans wanted a symbol for the new United States. Congress picked three people to design a seal. Thomas Jefferson, Ben Franklin, and John Adams drew a shield that had six parts. Each part showed a symbol of a different country. Together, the parts honored countries from which Americans had come. One of the six symbols was the eagle of Germany. Congress did not like the six-part shield.

2 Other groups drew seals. But Congress did not like their designs either. Then, in 1782, Charles Thomson and William Barton tried a new design. They drew one that featured a bald eagle. Congress liked this design and made it the Great Seal of the United States.

Symbol of a New Country

3   One familiar use of the Great Seal of the United States is on the back of a one-dollar bill. The bald eagle has its wings spread. It holds the arrows of war with its left talon. The olive branch of peace is in its right talon. This image shows that Congress alone holds the power of war and peace.

4   The cloud over the eagle's head stands for glory. Thirteen stars are in the cloud. They stand for the first thirteen states.

5   The eagle also has a shield over its chest. Look closely at the shield. Nothing is holding it up. This shows that the United States stands alone. The country must rely on its own strength to be independent.

6   The shield has thirteen stripes. Seven are white and six are red. The stripes stand for the thirteen original states. They are side by side to show unity. The ribbon in the eagle's beak speaks of unity too. It says *E Pluribus Unum.* In Latin, that means "Out of many, one."

7   The colors in the Great Seal of the United States are red, white, and blue. Red stands for courage. White is for purity, and blue is for justice.

8   The law protects the Great Seal of the United States. People can't use the seal to sell a product. If they do, they can face a $250 fine. They could even go to jail for six months.

Eagles and Countries

9   The United States was not the first country to use an eagle as its symbol. The Sumerians

[Soo•mair'•ee•uns] used it 5000 years ago. The ancient Romans used an eagle. Russia and Austria used it too. People think eagles look strong and brave.

A Lonely Voice

10   Not everyone liked the eagle as a symbol of the United States. Ben Franklin did not want to use it. He wanted a true North American bird instead. Eagles live in North America, but they also live in other parts of the world. Franklin liked the turkey better.

11   Franklin pointed out the eagle's bad habits. He saw the eagle as a lazy thief. It waits for some small bird to catch a fish. Then the eagle swoops down and steals it. Franklin praised his own choice. He said, "The turkey is a much more respectable bird. It is a true native of North America."

12   Ben Franklin died more than 200 years ago. Since then, leaders have used the eagle seal. But Franklin's bird also won a special place. Sadly for the turkey, that place is on the Thanksgiving table. In the meantime, the eagle flies high in American hearts.

Questions

1. When did the United States decide to make a seal?

2. Who designed the Great Seal?

3. What things are pictured on the Great Seal of the United States?

4. On the Great Seal, what do the colors red, white, and blue stand for?

Recognizing Stated Concepts

1. On the Great Seal, what is symbolized by the arrows and by the olive branch that the eagle holds?

2. What parts of the Great Seal stand for unity?

3. Why do people use eagles as symbols?

4. Why did Ben Franklin like the turkey better than the eagle?

The Chunnel Under the Sea

Why build a tunnel under the English Channel?

1　In one sense, England is part of Europe. English history is closely tied to that of Europe. The music and art of England have strong links with Europe. England also trades with all the nations of Europe.

2　　In another sense, England has not been part of Europe. After all, England is part of an island. The English Channel divides it from the rest of Europe. Getting from England to the rest of Europe and back has always required a boat or plane ride.

3　　That, however, is no longer true. A land route now links England to France. In 1994, the Channel Tunnel opened. Nicknamed the Chunnel, it is 31 miles long—the world's longest underwater tunnel.

An Old Idea

4　Before the last ice age, England was connected to France by land. When the ice melted, about 8000 years ago, the sea level rose and created the English Channel. That body of water made travel between England and Europe much more difficult than before.

5   By 1751, people were thinking about building a tunnel under the channel. In the early 1800s, Emperor Napoleon I of France made plans to build a dual tunnel. But war broke out and killed his dream.

6   Since then, other dreamers have wanted to build a tunnel. But people's fears on both sides of the channel always stopped them. Some people thought that armies might use such a tunnel to invade. Others worried that a tunnel would help the spread of disease.

7   At last, in 1986, such fears were put aside. People on both sides of the channel really wanted a tunnel. So the French and the English agreed to work together on the project. They figured that the tunnel would cost $7 billion. They planned to open the tunnel in 1993.

8   Building the tunnel was a huge project. New problems came up that surprised the planners. They had extra work to do. So, in the end, the Chunnel cost $16 billion. And it opened a year later than planned.

Building the Chunnel

9   It was a challenge to build such a tunnel. Engineers built special boring machines, called moles. These moles were huge. Each one weighed 1500 tons and was longer than two football fields. The machines

did the job—their massive blades made holes that were perfectly round. They dug out about 245 million cubic feet of earth. At one point, the moles dug 148 feet below the seabed of the English Channel.

10   One group of workers started in France. Another started in England. Their goal was to make the tunnels meet under the English Channel. When they did meet, in 1990, everyone was amazed. The meeting point of the tunnels was off the right measure by just eight inches.

11   The project took 10,000 workers to complete. Their job was wet, muddy, and cold. It was also dangerous. Eight English workers and two French workers died on the job. That safety record was not too bad. When Japan built the world's second-longest tunnel, 30 workers lost their lives.

The Chunnel Design

12   The Chunnel is really made up of three tunnels. Two of them have train tracks. The trains on one set of tracks run from England to France. The trains on the other set run from France to England. The third tunnel is a service tunnel with a road. Trucks use this third passageway to carry supplies and workers. The workers keep the other two tunnels in good shape.

13   The trains themselves are much larger than average-sized trains. In fact, they are the widest trains ever built. They need room enough to carry cars, buses, and trucks as well as people. Despite their size, these trains zip through the Chunnel at

nearly 90 miles per hour. The passenger trains are even faster. They go 186 miles per hour.

14   Two locomotives, one in the front and one in the back, run each train. Most locomotives have one engine. But each Chunnel locomotive has six of them. That totals twelve engines for each train!

15   There is a good reason for having many engines. Europe uses three different electric systems. So there has to be one engine for each. Each system also needs a second engine as a backup. No one wants to get stuck in the Chunnel because of a power failure.

Dealing with Problems

16 The Chunnel has had a few problems. One was heat. No one thought the tunnels would get hot. But the trains speeding back and forth made the tunnels very hot. So the builders had to add an air-conditioning system. This added another $200 million to the cost of the project. The new system is large enough to cool 6000 homes.

17   Some people worried about floods. They didn't want to drown if the Chunnel sprang a leak. Builders say there is really no danger of large leaks because the tunnel is far below the seabed. What's more, the tunnel walls are made of reinforced concrete and cast iron. Fire, however, is a more likely danger. Once again, the builders planned ahead. Any fire that breaks out will not spread. Automatic doors slam shut to contain the blaze. Then foam will spray on the fire to put it out.

The Way to Go

18 Is it faster to fly across the English Channel than to use the Chunnel? Yes, but the Chunnel is better able to carry people and cargo. Airports in London and Paris are far from the centers of those cities. They are often plagued by flight delays. Chunnel travelers can hop into their cars, drive onto a train, and be across the channel in 35 minutes. Or they can ride from downtown London to downtown Paris. The passenger train takes only three hours.

19   Each year more people use the Chunnel. Soon they will forget that it was once just a dream.

Questions

1. In what ways is England part of Europe?

2. What fears stopped people from building a tunnel sooner?

3. What were some of the problems that the builders of the Chunnel faced?

4. What have builders done to make the Chunnel safe and comfortable?

5. How is travel by the Chunnel better than travel by air?

Using Graphs and Maps

1. This article tells how much the Chunnel was expected to cost and how much it really cost. If you made a bar graph to compare these amounts, how many bars would you need? How would the bars be labeled? Where would you place the dollar figures? Now that you have decided on the design of the graph, draw the graph, using labels where they are needed.

2. Which of these topics would be best shown in a circle graph?
   a. the order of events in building the Chunnel
   b. how the total cost of the project was split up
   c. how the cost of the project grew, year by year

3. On a map, find London, Paris, and the English Channel. Use the scale to find
   a. the shortest distance between London and Paris, and
   b. the distance across the English Channel at its narrowest point.

4. Look at the map again. Why has there been little, if any, talk about building a tunnel from England to the Netherlands?

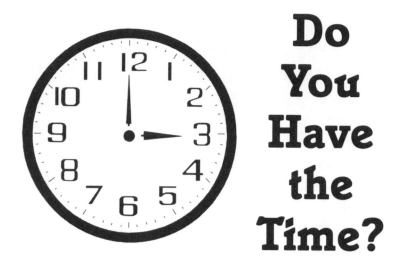

Do You Have the Time?

How did people run their lives before there were clocks?

1 From the moment you wake up in the morning to the time you go to bed at night, you run your life by the clock. All day long, you check the time. A little clock on your wrist always lets you know what time it is. Without a wristwatch, you'd have to stop someone and ask, "Do you have the time?"

2 It's hard to think of a world without clocks. Yet people have worn wristwatches for only the last 100 years. And until 300 years ago, most people did not have clocks in their homes. They did not think about time the way we do today.

Living by the Sun

3 Before the invention of clocks, people used the sun to tell time. In the morning, they rose with the sun. And they went to bed when the sun went down. During the day, if the sun was shining, they could tell the time by looking at shadows.

4   In these early times, people did not divide the day into hours. For them, the parts of a day were sunrise, noon, and sunset. Night was just night.

5   The first invention used for telling time was the sundial. It came into use about 4000 years ago, around 2000 B.C. The face of a sundial is marked off in hours. In the middle, a raised piece makes a shadow. During the day, the shadow moves across the marks to tell the hours. Of course, a sundial works only when the sun shines. But a sundial that is accurate in the summer is not accurate in the winter. The Earth tilts as the seasons change. This causes the sun to be in a different position at a given hour in a winter sky than at that same hour in a summer sky. So a sundial that correctly tells the hour as 3 o'clock in the summer might tell the same hour as 2 o'clock in the winter.

Early Ideas

6   People tried other methods of telling time besides using the sundial. One method used a rope with knots in it. The space between each two knots was the same. The rope was set on fire at one end. Each knot that burned stood for another hour gone by. How well do you think that worked? A better idea was the use of a candle marked in pieces from top to bottom. Each marked piece that melted stood for an hour.

7   Even better for measuring time was the hourglass. An hourglass has two glass balls, one on top of the other, with a tiny hole between them. It takes one hour for sand to flow from one ball into the other. Then the hourglass is turned upside

down to measure another hour. The ancient Greeks used an hourglass when a person running for office was making a speech. Maybe this is what is meant by the saying "Your time is running out."

The Water Clock

8 Another kind of clock used water. A water clock made in 1400 B.C. had a clay bowl with dots inside. The dots marked the hours as water slowly dripped out the bowl's bottom. Around 400 B.C., ancient Greeks improved the water clock. They used a glass jar with the hours painted on the outside. Like earlier clocks, it was used to time speeches.

9   None of these clocks worked very well. But no one could think of a better one for another 1500 years. Most people went right on telling time by the sun.

The Mechanical Clock

10 At last, around the year A.D. 1300, the mechanical clock was invented. Its gears and wheels ran by a weight on a long chain. As the weight pulled down on the chain, a drum turned. The drum turned the gears. A hook caught onto teeth in the gears. This kept the weight from going down too fast. That action made the "ticktock" sound in a clock. This kind of clock was hung in church towers. It had no face or hands. A bell rang to tell the hours.

Some Progress

11 In the late 1300s, clocks began to have dials. But there was only one hand, which told the hours. These clocks did not keep good time. At noon, on sunny

days, someone had to reset the clock according to a sundial. The sun was still the best clock!

12   In the 1500s, people began to use a spring, not a weight, to run the clock. This meant they could wind up the clock. They could also make the clock smaller. In those days, a watchman walked through the city at night. He wore a small clock that hung from a strap around his neck. People started to call the watchman's clock a watch.

13   In 1657, the pendulum clock was invented. A pendulum swinging back and forth helped keep the time.

Getting Clock Wise

14   By the 1700s, mechanical clocks were everywhere. People now ran their lives by the clock instead of the sun. Men carried pocket watches. In the 1800s, wristwatches were invented. But they were made only for women! During World War I (1914–1918), soldiers saw how handy it was to wear a wristwatch. After that, both men and women wore them.

15   Electric clocks came into the home around 1920. Quartz clocks were made as early as the 1930s. In the 1940s came atomic clocks. They can tell the time to within one second in 100 years! And digital clocks arrived in the 1970s.

16   People once lived their lives by the sun. Today, we run our lives by the clock. And we will likely find better and fancier ways to tell time. But no matter how we measure it, time marches on—and waits for no one.

Questions

1. What was the first invention for telling time?

2. Why is a sundial that is accurate in the summer not as accurate in the winter?

3. About what year was the mechanical clock invented?

4. Describe one of the changes made to the mechanical clock that helped it keep better time.

Using Forms and Schedules

1. Pretend that you are ordering a grandfather clock from a catalog. Make an order form that shows the billing address, shipping address, item quantity, description, price, sales tax, shipping and handling charge, and payment method.

2. For a week, keep a schedule of your daily activities, noting how much time you spend on each. How does the amount of your leisure time during the week compare with the amount on the weekend? Do you sleep more during the week or on the weekend?

3. Use a time zone map to compare times around the world. Pick a city in Europe and compare times on your daily schedule with times in that city. What time is it there when you wake up, leave for school, eat lunch, and so on?

The History of Money

Which world leader was the first to have his picture stamped on each new coin made?

1 Let's suppose that you would like to have a new pair of shoes and there is no such thing as money. You do, however, have a field full of corn. You pick some corn and take it to the person who makes shoes. You offer to trade a pair of shoes for the corn. The shoemaker agrees, and you go home with a new pair of shoes. You have just taken part in a barter.

2 But suppose that the shoemaker has all the corn he needs right now. What he really wants is some nails for making shoes. So first you go to the nail maker and trade your corn for nails. You then take the nails to the shoemaker and trade them for new shoes.

Time and Trouble

3 This story shows how barter works. It also shows that bartering for everything you need could take a

lot of time and trouble. Yet that is how people once traded for all goods and services.

4   Bartering could be much more trying than this story shows. Long ago, members of your tribe or family would bring what they had to trade to a certain place at a certain time. They would lay down their goods, then hide. Another family or tribe would then lay down *their* goods. Then they would hide as well. Your group would come out and look at what the other group had left. If you thought it made a fair trade, you would take their things and leave yours for them to take. Let's say it was not a fair trade. You would take away some of your goods and hide again. The other group would then come out and look at what was left. This could go on and on until both groups felt they had a fair trade.

Setting a Standard

5   There had to be a better way. Why not have one kind of thing to use for trading? People would know its set value. It would be a standard item that people could use to buy exactly what they needed. Goods and services would have prices. A certain amount of the item chosen could be used to pay those prices.

6   The first "money" was cows. Tribes kept cows to trade for what they needed. Around 3000 B.C., people started using other things for money. Gold, silver, honey, oil, wine, and wool were some of the things used. Money made trading simple and clear to everyone.

7   We know about early forms of money from the kinds of objects found in the ground that were lost or buried by people of long ago. Arrowheads made from good stone have been found in Japan. Fishhooks made of pearl have surfaced in New Guinea. Fine copper knives have been found in China. Stone axes too small for real use have been found in Europe. People once used these and other things as money. In fact, heaps of such things have been found. These piles of goods may have been the first banks.

Gold and Silver

8 Still, people needed yet a better way to buy and sell. Some people used pieces of gold as money. The gold's value was based on its weight. But it was not always easy to weigh the gold before spending it.

9   Coins were first used about 900 B.C. Round, flat pieces of metal have been found near the Black Sea in Asia. The coins were made of gold and silver mixed together. A coin's value was based on its weight or on the number of coins used. People who had something to sell made the first coins. But it didn't take long for governments to take over the job of making money.

10   Around 700 B.C., a new way of making money began. After coins were struck in metal, they were stamped with a picture or pattern. Later, a machine called a punch "punched" the picture on both sides of the coin. In early Greece, silver coins carried the picture of a person's head or an owl.

11   Alexander the Great took gold and silver from the lands he won. He brought it home to Greece and turned it into coins. They could be used anywhere in the country. This was the first large, public money system. When Alexander the Great died, his picture was placed on every new coin made.

Paper Money

12   The first paper money came from China. Marco Polo sent reports of these bills back to Europe from his trips. The money was made of bark from the mulberry tree. The bills were large, about the size of today's typing paper. Different sizes stood for different values. But the Chinese soon stopped using paper money. It was too easy to copy.

13   To conserve gold and silver, King Henry VIII of England coated copper coins with silver. He put his own picture on the coins. With a little wear, however, the silver rubbed off and made the king's nose red. People started calling the king "Old Copper Nose."

14   When the Spanish first came to the New World, they found gold coins in use. They took a great deal of gold back to Europe. They melted it down to make their own gold coins. Other Europeans found that North American Indians used wampum as money. This was a string of small shell beads.

Modern Methods

15   Back in Europe, some countries started making paper "notes." These notes were not real money. They only stood for money. A goldsmith or a bank

held the gold or silver for which the paper stood. The notes were much easier to carry around than coins.

16   The early government in America made paper money, too. But these bills were not backed by gold or silver. And, as the Chinese had learned, paper money was too easily copied. So the government stopped making it. Paper money did not come into common use in the United States until the Civil War, in the 1860s. Today, special ink and special paper are used. People still try to copy money, but now it's much harder to do.

Money Today

17   Today, only coins and paper are used as money. And none of it has real gold or silver behind it. Checks, credit cards, and "money" cards act as notes. They stand for the real money being held in a bank or some kind of account. We can buy and sell without ever touching a coin or bill. That has its problems, but it beats trading corn for a new pair of shoes!

Questions

1. Describe the way people first made a typical fair trade.

2. What standard item was the first early form of money?

3. When did coins come into use?

4. Which country made the first paper money?

5. Which ruler was nicknamed "Old Copper Nose"? Why?

Understanding Consumer Materials

1. Find two advertisements for the same product, such as a CD player or television, in a newspaper. Compare prices, payment options, and finance charges. Then write a paragraph explaining which one is a better buy.

2. Find an car advertisement that offers a finance plan. Calculate the total cost of the car using the finance plan offered by the dealer. How much more does a car bought on time cost than one that is purchased outright?

3. Prepare a weekly food budget and a meal plan. Use the food section of the newspaper to make a shopping list. See how closely you can stay within your budget while purchasing food for the week's meals.

Coretta Scott King: The Dream Lives On

Why has Coretta Scott King won a place in the hearts of many Americans?

1   Coretta Scott King is a special woman. She was married to one of the great civil rights leaders of all time, Dr. Martin Luther King, Jr. Coretta Scott King helped him in many ways and was often at his side. After King's death, she became a leader in her own right.

Early Years

2   Coretta Scott was born in Alabama in 1927. Her father ran a small store. The store did not bring in enough money to support the family. To make ends meet, Coretta's father hauled lumber as a second job. Her mother worked, too, driving a school bus. Even young Coretta pitched in. She picked cotton to earn money.

3   In some ways, life was hard for Coretta. Each day she had to walk five miles to school. Harder still was the sight of a school bus passing her by. The bus was filled with white children. Because Coretta was African American, she was not allowed to ride the bus. Such unfair treatment stung her. Someday, she vowed, people would treat her as an equal.

A Good Education

4   All the students in Coretta's high school were African American. Some of the teachers were white, and others were black. These teachers were the first college graduates that Coretta had known. She saw that people with education had more choices in life. They were treated with respect. Coretta decided that going to college would improve her life.

5   Coretta studied hard to make her dream come true. She finished first in her high school class and went on to Antioch College in Yellow Springs, Ohio. Coretta studied to be a teacher but also took courses in music. She had a lovely voice and played the piano with ease.

Career Choices

6   Coretta did well in college. But when it was time to do some practice teaching, she had a letdown. Antioch students always did their practice teaching at the Yellow Springs public schools. But no African American had ever taught in the public schools. So Coretta was sent to the school run by the college.

7   Coretta's race had become an issue once again. It kept her from getting the same training that her white classmates got. Coretta decided not to become a teacher after all. She went on with her studies in music. After college, Coretta moved to Boston and enrolled in a top music school. She did not have much money. For a time, she lived on graham crackers, peanut butter, and fruit. Still, she was happy to be doing something she loved.

Fighting for Equal Rights

8   In Boston, Coretta met Martin Luther King, Jr., who was also a student. The two of them talked about their hopes for the future. Their goals in life were very much the same. Both Scott and King wanted to help African Americans win equal rights. They hoped to end the suffering that came from racial prejudice [prej'•uh•dis].

9   In 1953, Scott and King married. The next year, when they finished school, they moved to Alabama. The year after that, the first of their four children was born. In 1956, King helped launch a bus boycott in Montgomery, Alabama. The goal was to end poor treatment of blacks on city buses. The boycott went on for a year. By the time it ended, King was famous. From then on, he was a leader in the civil rights movement.

Living with Danger

10   King's work stirred the feelings of many white people. Some of them agreed with him, but others did not. A few of King's enemies even wanted to

get rid of him. One day someone threw a bomb at the King home. Luckily, no one was hurt. But it was clear that the King family was a target for angry whites.

11 Over the next 12 years, Coretta Scott King feared for the safety of her family. Still, she and her husband went on with their civil rights work. King was in the public eye more and more. He gave speeches and set up marches. Through the years, Coretta often marched beside her husband. She sometimes spoke in his place when he had to miss a speaking date. On tours of the United States and abroad, she was at King's side. At the meetings, she often sang about civil rights. In 1964, Coretta talked about her family's life. She knew they lived "on the edge of danger." She said, "People constantly ask Martin and me how we can hope to raise normal, healthy and happy children. . . ." Her answer was simple. She said, "I can only answer that we have faith in God and that we try to be good parents."

Carrying On

12 On April 4, 1968, Martin Luther King, Jr., was shot and killed. Coretta bravely carried on her husband's work. She gave the speeches that he had planned to give. She took his place at a march planned long before.

13 To honor his memory, Coretta created the King Center. It includes King's childhood home and his tomb. The Atlanta church where King worked is also part of the center.

14   More than three million people visit the King Center each year. Although the center has kept Coretta busy, she has found time for other human rights work. She has spoken at peace rallies. She has also given many freedom concerts. Her words and songs keep alive the struggle against racism, poverty, and war. In 1994, she led a march on Washington, D.C., just as her husband had done more than 30 years before.

15   By her words and actions, Coretta Scott King has won a place in the hearts of many Americans. People will always remember her as the wife of Martin Luther King, Jr. But she will also be honored for her own strength, grace, and dignity.

Questions

1. Why did Coretta Scott move to Boston?

2. What dreams did Coretta Scott and Martin Luther King, Jr., share?

3. What did Coretta Scott King do after her husband's death?

Analyzing Characters/Identifying Main Idea

1. What problems did Coretta Scott face as a young girl? How did these problems affect her?

2. What character traits helped Coretta Scott King continue her work for civil rights after her husband's death?

3. This article has six parts. What is provided to point out the main idea in each of the parts?

4. What is the main idea of the selection as a whole?

What We Know About Memory

Can a person's memory improve?

1 What did you have for dinner last Friday? Who won last year's Super Bowl? Can you name your childhood friends? Don't be surprised if you can't. No one's memory is perfect.

Not a Simple System

2 Scientists don't know just how memory works. But the brain stores facts in a complex way. First the information goes deep into the brain. Then it is stored as part of a pattern. These patterns lie in different parts of the brain.

3 So far, the system sounds clear. But the patterns are not. For example, nouns are stored away from verbs. The brain stores the names of things made by people in one place. But the names of natural things, like plants, are stored in another. No one has found out why this is so.

Making Memories

4 Some memories are stronger than others right from the start. You will have stronger memories of things you think are important. It is easier to remember things learned right before going to sleep. And you will remember happy times better than sad ones.

5 What do you know right now? It's easy to learn more about things you know already. Your brain lets you link one memory with another. For example, pretend that you and a friend read the same book. It is about a famous dancer. Before reading the book, your friend knows nothing about dance. But you know a great deal about it.

6 Your friend will have a hard time remembering facts from the book. Your friend's brain has no special place for dance facts. But your prior knowledge will help you remember what you read. You can connect new facts with old ones. Hooking new facts onto the old ones makes stronger memories.

Words to Remember

7 Many experts say that there are five types of memory. One type includes all the words you know, even ones you haven't used in years. It also includes symbols. A dollar sign and the logo of a sports team are symbols. This type of memory also helps you remember basic traits of things. An example would be the difference between the look of a cat and that of a dog.

8 This kind of memory is hard to lose. This is true even of people with Alzheimer's [alts'•hi•murz]

disease. They may lose most of their other kinds of memory. But about half of them hang on to this kind.

Other Types of Memory

9 A second type of memory has to do with physical skills. Tying your shoe, for example, uses this kind of memory. You don't stop and think about each movement. Yet your hands do the right things in the right order.

10 A third type of memory is made up of facts. This kind holds things learned at school. It also stores things learned from movies, books, and friends. Quiz-show winners are people who remember facts well.

11 The shortest-term memory type lasts only a few seconds. It deals with what is going on at the moment. It remembers the start of a sentence while the speaker gets to its end. It also lets people do several things at once. You use short-term memory when you talk and watch TV while keeping your train of thought.

12 The last type of memory concerns events from your recent past. These are memories of what you wore yesterday and where you ate lunch. As people age, these memories fade the most.

Sharpen Your Wits

13 Older people tend to forget things easily. But people of all ages want to remember things better. Some wish they could recall the names of people they meet. Others want to do well on a test. Still

others complain that they forget birthdays or lunch dates.

14   The good news is that you can improve your memory. One way is called reinforcement. Try this. The next time you meet someone, say his or her name. Use the name several times as you talk with that person. This practice will create a stronger memory of the name.

15   You can also exercise your brain. Just as exercise tones the muscles, learning improves the mind. Take a course in something you like. Study a second language. Even time spent with quick-thinking people might sharpen your wits.

16   Many people rely on memory aids, or mnemonics [nih•mon'•iks]. One aid is a word whose letters stand for things you want to remember. To remember the names of the Great Lakes, for example, use HOMES. Each letter stands for the name of one of the five lakes.

17   No system is foolproof—people will still forget things. Maybe someday there will be a memory pill. In the meantime, just look up the winner of last year's game. You may *never* remember what you had for dinner last Friday!

Questions

1. How do scientists think the brain stores memories?

2. What are the five types of memory?

3. Name two ways to improve your memory.

Comparing and Contrasting/Drawing Conclusions

1. Which type of memory fades the most over time—words and symbols or events from the recent past?

2. What type of memory does riding a bicycle use? How is that type of memory different from short-term memory?

3. Why does prior knowledge of a subject help you remember new facts about that subject?

4. How does learning a new language help improve your memory?

Black Soldiers: Unsung Heroes

How did black soldiers help save the Union during the Civil War?

1 The Civil War, fought between 1861 and 1865, threatened to break up the United States. It began as a struggle over states' rights. But in 1863, President Abraham Lincoln changed history. He made the war a fight to end slavery. Black soldiers played a key role in this fight.

Not Wanted

2 Most people felt that a war would end in a few weeks or months. Some free black men offered to join the Union army. But they were turned down. Union leaders did not think the army needed them.

3 The hope of a short war ended soon after the Battle of Bull Run. The North lost this battle, fought three months after the war started. Such defeat meant that the war could last for years. Still, there was no call for blacks to join the army. Northern

leaders were sure that white soldiers could win the war alone.

Black Volunteers

4 If the army wouldn't have them, maybe blacks could help the cause in other ways. In large numbers, they stepped forward to do many kinds of work. They built roads and forts. They carried supplies to the front lines. In short, these volunteers did whatever they could to help the Union cause.

5 But blacks were still not allowed to fight for the Union. That rule began to change in 1862. The war had been going badly for the North. In Kansas, a white abolitionist [ab•uh•lish'•uh•nist] named Jim Lane took action. He set up two black regiments. Even though they were not part of the regular Union army, they fought bravely in two small battles. "[The black soldiers] fought like tigers," said one Southerner.

Fighting for Freedom

6 On New Year's Day 1863, President Abraham Lincoln issued his Emancipation Proclamation [ih•man•suh•pay'•shun prok•luh•may'•shun]. It was a bold move. It freed the slaves in the South. That, by itself, meant little. Since the war was still going on, Lincoln could not force the South to obey. But in another sense, the proclamation meant everything. It gave the Civil War an added purpose: the fight was now to end slavery.

7 The proclamation also allowed black men to join the Union army. Black soldiers could now fight in

separate units under white officers. Many blacks rushed to join the army. They wanted to fight for freedom. Those who were already free fought to end slavery for other blacks. Still others who joined the Union side were slaves who had run away. They fought so that they would never again be slaves.

Black Soldiers in Action

8   Nearly 200,000 black soldiers fought for the Union army. They fought in 39 large battles and in hundreds of small ones. They fought in all parts of the country. Blacks also served in the Navy. In fact, one out of four sailors was black.

9   One famous Civil War battle took place in South Carolina. A black regiment called the 54th Massachusetts attacked Fort Wagner in July 1863. The battle was a bloody defeat for the 54th. Against heavy odds, the soldiers fought bravely. In spite of their courage, more than 1500 blacks were killed. One black soldier, William H. Carney, carried the regiment's flag. He was shot several times but never dropped the banner he held proudly. Carney was later given the Medal of Honor. He was one of 16 black soldiers to win this medal during the Civil War.

10   Black soldiers fought in many other bloody battles as well. At Port Hudson, Louisiana, more than 600 of them died. Many more were killed at Fort Pillow, Tennessee. Only a few survived the vicious [vish′•us] fighting there. At Petersburg, Virginia, a black unit got trapped while trying to rescue a white unit. Many blacks died in the struggle.

Unfair Treatment

11   Black soldiers were paid about half of what white soldiers of the same rank earned. They felt that the separate pay rates were unfair. "[Are] we soldiers," they asked, "or are we laborers? We have done a soldier's duty. Why can't we have a soldier's pay?"

12   General Ben Butler agreed with that thinking. "The [black man] fills an equal space in the ranks while he lives," said Butler, "and an equal grave when he falls." In 1864, the Union granted equal pay to all soldiers.

13   In all, 37,638 black soldiers died during the Civil War. It was a huge sacrifice of human life. As Lincoln said, the Union could not have won the war without the black soldiers. And slavery would not have ended without that victory.

Questions

1. Early in the war, what did blacks do to help the Union cause?

2. How did the Emancipation Proclamation change the purpose of the war?

3. What happened at Fort Wagner, South Carolina, in July 1863?

4. About how many blacks fought for the Union during the Civil War? About how many died in the war?

Identifying Cause and Effect/ Summarizing and Paraphrasing/ Finding Supporting Evidence

1. Why did the Union army turn away black volunteers at first?

2. Why were blacks finally allowed to fight for the Union forces?

3. In your own words, tell how black soldiers in the Union army felt about their pay rate prior to 1864.

4. Find two sentences that support the idea that black soldiers helped save the Union during the Civil War.

A Walk Through the Rain Forest

How is a rain forest different from any other forest?

1 Imagine a place with a water plant that has leaves large enough to hold a child. Next to it is a flower three feet wide. It looks and smells like rotten meat. Nearby is a frog so big it can eat a rat.

2 The forest is thick—so thick that sunlight never reaches the ground. Imagine trees 200 feet tall. They need the support of vines to keep them from falling over. The many forest plants grow not on the ground but on top of other plants.

3 This seems like a scene from a wild dream. But it is the everyday look of a rain forest. Rain forests are very much like jungles. They grow in the middle parts of the world, where the weather is the warmest. Think of a band or belt around Earth. Places within this band are Central America and the northern part of South America. Parts of Africa, India, and Southeast Asia also form this belt of rain forests. Still other lands within this area are the East

and West Indies and the island of Madagascar [mad•uh•gas'•kur], as well as some parts of Australia and the Philippines.

Hot and Humid

4   Rain forests need warm weather and plenty of rain. The temperature in a rain forest is always around 80 degrees. Rain falls for several hours each day and totals 8 to 10 inches in one month. India set a record for rainfall in 1860. That year, 86 feet of rain fell! With such hot and humid weather, a house built in a rain forest will last only about five years.

5   The rain forest recycles its rain. A big tree pumps out about 200 gallons of water a day from its leaves. This moisture turns into clouds, which drop the water to Earth again as rain. The tree roots suck up the water, and the cycle begins again.

6   The rain forest also recycles its food. In other kinds of forests, dead leaves fall and pile up. They turn to dirt slowly, letting the soil become deep and rich. But in a rain forest, leaves and branches fall to earth. In the heat and moisture, they quickly rot and become food for the forest plants. But the plants take in the nutrients in the food right away. So the soil in a rain forest never has a chance to build up. It is only an inch or two thick!

A Different Look

7   In soil so thin, trees do not form deep roots. Instead, the trees sprout side roots that help prop them up. Without these roots, tall trees easily fall over. Long, thick vines grow into the tree branches. The vines tie the trees together and also help hold them up.

8   The largest trees of the rain forest put everything else there into shade. Below these tall trees lies open forest. The dim light creates the feeling of being in a huge church with a ceiling about 17 stories high! Ferns and other plants grow on the forest floor. It is too dark for young trees to grow. But a fallen tree or big, broken branch leaves a hole in the "roof." Young trees can then grow quickly, each racing to fill the hole.

A Healthy Blend

9   In the warm, wet climate of the rain forest, plants grow quickly. Bamboo has the fastest growth rate. It is really a kind of grass and can grow three feet in a single day. A bamboo plant may become 100 feet tall. Other plants, called air plants, grow on the high branches of trees. They take in moisture from the damp air. One big tree may hold thousands of these plants. The plants may get so heavy that the tree branches break off.

10   A rain forest has the widest variety of plants and animals in the world. A few acres could include 42,000 kinds of insects, 750 kinds of trees, and 1,500 other plant types. Covering just one square yard of the forest might be 800 ants of 50 different kinds.

11   Why are the rain forests so important to us? One reason is our need for their rich blend of plants and animals. Rain forests contain more than half the world's known plant and animal varieties. They may hold others we have yet to discover. Rain forests may be the source of new, life-saving medicines. They may also hold better kinds of plants for use as food. These forests are important

also because they improve the quality of air. As trees put moisture into the air, they also clean it.

Upsetting Mother Nature

12   But the rain forests of the world are in danger. Farmers need land for growing crops, so they cut down and burn a part of a rain forest. The thin, shallow soil of the forest is hard to farm. After a few years, the farmers give up on that land. So they cut down another part of the forest to try for better farmland. Across the world, 82,000 acres of trees are cut down each day.

13   Cutting down the forests makes many kinds of plants and animals die out completely. The thin soil of a rain forest washes away easily, so the trees can never grow back. We will lose forever about a million kinds of plants and animals by the beginning of the 21st century.

14   Cutting down and burning the rain forests creates other problems. Losing forests in the middle part of the world may cause weather changes for all of Earth. Air filled with the smoke of burning trees replaces clean, moist air the trees once gave off. The large amounts of smoke may worsen the air worldwide.

15   Losing the forests upsets the balance of nature in yet another way. When it rains, the trees soak up the water. Without the trees, rainwater runs off the bare ground and causes flooding.

16   In 20 or 30 years, the world's rain forests may be gone completely. It seems that they are being destroyed for nothing.

Questions

1. List some places where rain forests are found.

2. Which rain forest plant grows fastest?

3. Why is the soil so thin in a rain forest?

4. Why are so many rain forests destroyed?

5. How could cutting down a rain forest cause flooding?

Predicting Outcomes/Identifying Fact and Opinion

1. Write a paragraph predicting the effect that cutting down and burning the rain forests might have on world weather.

2. Do you think the benefits of clearing forests for farming outweigh the damage to the environment? Or do you oppose losing rain forest to farming? Write a letter to the editor expressing your opinion.

3. Reread the article and find five facts about the rain forest.

How to Survive Anything

Can you keep your cool in the face of danger?

1 It's a dangerous world out there. Life is full of close calls. You might some day find yourself in one of the following jams. Here are ways to make it through in one piece—with a smile on your face.

Calm a Mad Dog

2 You're out walking. You hear the bark of an angry dog behind you.

The Basics

3 1. Animals are not kind.
4 2. If you panic, they panic.
5 3. If they panic, they bite.

The Details

6 *You will want to run.* Don't. Almost two million people are bitten by dogs each year. You can't outrun most dogs. Most of the time, the dog is

angry because you are on its turf. It is trying to
scare you off.

7 *Play on the dog's terms.* Stand still. Turn and face the
dog. Don't make any quick movements. Talk in a
quiet voice. This shows the dog you're not a threat.
The dog should calm down. When it does, back
away slowly. Keep watching the dog.

8 *Throw the dog a bone.* Do you have some food in
your pocket? Share it. The old saying is true—a dog
is not likely to bite the hand that feeds it.

9 *What if this doesn't work?* If the dog doesn't calm
down, try to show it you're the boss. Stand as tall
as you can. Scream and stare it in the eye. Take off
your jacket or sweater. Wrap it around your fist. If
the dog comes at you, offer your protected fist.
Back off slowly, taking the dog with you. When
you reach a safe place, let go of the clothing.

10 What if the dog is a strong one, such as a
Doberman, and you don't think you can fight it
off? Curl into a ball with your hands over your
head. The dog may still bite you. But your throat
and other vital parts are protected.

Make It Through a Storm at Sea

11 There's an old joke about getting seasick: First you're
afraid you're going to die. Then you're afraid you
won't. From birth, people are used to solid ground.
A rocking boat throws the system off balance.

The Basics

12 1. Go with the motion of the ocean.

13 2. Don't eat greasy foods before you sail.

14 3. Stay in the middle of the boat.

The Details

15 *Deny everything.* Don't worry about getting seasick, and there's a good chance you won't.

16 *Watch what you eat.* Don't eat a lot before boarding the boat. Stick with mild foods like crackers. Drink plenty of water, and avoid alcohol and greasy foods.

17 *Never go below.* Stay on deck. If you go below, the room will seem to be standing still. But your sense of balance will tell you you're moving. That can make you seasick.

18 *Eat ginger.* Ginger seems to soothe the stomach. Try ginger ale or ginger tablets or even ginger snaps.

19 *Take medicine early.* You can buy medicine at the drugstore to prevent seasickness. But it will help only if you take it before you feel sick. There is a patch you can wear to prevent seasickness. But your doctor must prescribe it for you.

Escape a Towering Inferno

20 It's fun to watch a disaster movie. But nobody wants to star in his or her own disaster. If you're in a tall building that catches fire, there are a few things you need to know.

The Basics

21 1. Stay out of elevators.

22 2. Stay down low.

23 3. Close the door against fire.

The Details

24 *Plan your getaway.* The tall building may be the office you go to every day. Or it may be your apartment house. It may even be a hotel you are

visiting. Find out where the fire escapes are. Hotels have maps in every room. Most offices and apartments also have maps. Plan at least two ways to get out. If you're in a hotel, count the room doors between your room and the fire escape. If the fire happens at night and you can't see, this will help you find your way.

25 *Step lively.* Get out as quickly as you can. Use smoke-free stairways. Never use the elevator.

26 *Lie low.* If a room or hall is full of smoke, crawl on your hands and knees. The best air is 12 to 24 inches from the floor. You can also see better there. If you can, put a wet cloth over your mouth and nose. This will help filter out the smoke.

27 *If you're trapped.* If you're trapped in a room, call the fire department. Tell them where you are. If the phones are out, get a flashlight and signal from the window. Or you can hang a light-colored sheet or towel out the window. Fill the bathtub with water. Soak towels in the water. Stuff them in cracks around the door and seal vents with them. Turn off any fans or air conditioners.

Stop Yourself from Choking

28 Choking is not the way a person expects to die. But it kills people more often than you think. If you get something stuck in your windpipe, don't wait around for help.

The Basics

29 All you need to know is how to do the Heimlich maneuver [hime'•lick muh•noo'•vur]. First make a fist. Put the thumb side against your upper

abdomen [ab'•duh•mun] just below your rib cage.
Hold the fist with your other hand. Push hard in
and up at the same time. The food should fly out of
your mouth.

30   If that doesn't work, lean over the back of a
chair. The edge should stick into your abdomen.
Push yourself quickly down on it. This should force
the air out of your diaphragm [die'•uh•fram]. Do
this until the pieces of food shoot out of your
mouth.

Avoid a Car Accident

31 You don't want to look ahead and see a car coming
across the road at you. But head-on crashes kill
5000 people a year in the United States.

The Basics

32 1. Swerve right! Quick!
33 2. A rear-end crash is better than one head-on.

The Details

34 *Light up.* Drive with your headlights on during the
day. Studies show that it helps prevent head-on
crashes.

35 *Avoid skidding.* Take your foot off the brake. Steer
away from trouble. At speeds higher than 30 miles
an hour, it is quicker to steer around something
than to stop your car. It is usually safer to steer to
the right. That is because the oncoming driver will
most often steer to his or her right.

36 *Crash straight ahead.* You may not be able to avoid
some kind of accident. If you must, hit someone

driving in the same direction as you are. It will be a less messy accident.

37 *Bounce back.* If you can't avoid hitting a tree or a guardrail, try to hit it with the side of your car.

38 *Use seat belts.* Wearing a seat belt is one of the best ways to protect yourself in a crash. This keeps you in the correct position behind the wheel.

If Your Brakes Give Out. . .

39 1. Pump them once or twice. See if you have any braking power.

40 2. If you don't have any brakes, put the car in neutral. Keep your eyes on the road ahead. Slow the car with the parking brake. If your parking brake is next to the driver's seat, keep your finger on the brake-release button. Slowly raise the brake. If your parking brake is on the floor, keep your left hand on the brake-release lever. Slowly press down with your foot.

41 3. If that doesn't work, steer to an open field. Or let your tires rub against the curb to slow you down.

42   Life is not certain, to say the least. But with a plan, some common sense, and a little luck, you *can* survive just about anything.

Questions

1. Why do you suppose the article began with the danger of an angry dog rather than any of the other dangers?

2. What should you do if you can't fight off a strong dog?

3. Name two things you shouldn't eat or drink before boarding a boat.

4. If you are trapped in a room of a building on fire, why would you soak towels in water?

5. In trying to avoid a head-on car crash, in which direction should you swerve?

Recognizing Author's Purpose/Making Generalizations

1. What is the author's purpose for writing this article?

2. After reading the hints for handling seasickness, what general statement can you make about avoiding becoming ill when you must travel by water?

3. When dealing with different kinds of danger, what general rule should you follow?

Tea: To Your Health

Is tea just a refreshing drink, or is it something more?

1 Tea is the most popular drink in the world—after water, that is. About half the people in the world drink tea. The Chinese have been brewing the stuff for 5000 years.

2 People drink tea mainly because they enjoy its taste. Now it seems there is one more good reason to drink it. Tea may be good for your health.

A Brief History of Tea

3 Who drank the first cup of tea? As the story goes, it was a Chinese philosopher [fih•los'•uh•fur]. He was boiling some water on a fire. A few tea leaves fell from a tree into the pot. The brew smelled so good that he drank a cup of it. Ever since then, tea has been the main drink in China.

4 Though the Chinese had tea for thousands of years, people in other places didn't. Tea reached

some parts of the world just a few hundred years
ago.

5   Europe got its first tea in 1610. Dutch traders
carried it from China. But most Europeans
[yur•uh•pee'•unz] liked coffee better. Only
England became a country of tea drinkers.
Drinking five or more cups a day is normal for an
English person. England buys more tea from the
countries that grow it than any other country does.

6   Early colonists brought tea with them to
America. At that time, the British government ruled
the colonies. In 1773, the government wanted more
money from the settlers. So it put a high tax on tea.
Colonists got so angry that they dumped all the tea
into Boston Harbor. After that event, called the
Boston Tea Party, colonists started to drink coffee.
Most Americans continue to be coffee drinkers.

The Three Teas

7 There are many kinds of tea leaves. But there are
only three ways to prepare them. In the end, the
leaves will be either green tea, black tea, or oolong
[oo'•long] tea.

8   To make green tea, workers steam the leaves in
large tubs, or vats. They then dry and crush the
leaves. Steaming the leaves keeps them from
changing color. It also destroys certain chemicals in
the leaves.

9   To make black tea, workers partly dry the leaves
on racks. They then crush them to take out the
flavorful juices. The leaves then go into a special
room called a fermenting room. Here the leaves are

dried in ovens. While the leaves go through these steps, they become nearly black in color.

10   Oolong tea falls between green tea and black tea in color and taste. Workers do not let this tea ferment as long as black tea does. So its color is not as dark.

Green Tea: A "Hot" Item

11 Green tea is a "hot"—or very exciting—item. The reason is that many scientists believe green tea may prevent some health problems.

12   When black and oolong teas are made, chemicals called GTPs are destroyed. Scientists now think GTPs are good for human beings. They fed green tea leaves to rats. When tested later, these rats had less heart disease than usual. They also had less cancer.

13   Scientists wondered if green tea would help humans in the same way. The answer seems to be yes. Green tea can help prevent the worst kinds of cancers in humans. Among these are cancers of the liver, lungs, and colon. The tea may also kill some stomach viruses and help prevent certain blood problems. It also stops tooth decay.

14   Scientists also know that green tea helps people with multiple sclerosis [mul'•tuh•pul skluh•row'•sis] (MS). The muscles of people with MS grow so weak that the people can't move or breathe. The Japanese don't have nearly as much MS as people in some other places. Scientists know that the Japanese drink a lot of green tea. So they get more GTPs than most people do. This may be helping them to stay healthy.

Benefits of Black Tea

15 Black tea may also be good for you. Tests with mice showed that it prevented skin cancer. Scientists put mice under the light rays that cause skin cancer. Some mice were fed black tea. Others got green tea or water. The mice that drank the black tea had fewer skin cancers. The scientists now hope to show that black tea can help humans too.

Possible Dangers

16 So should you drink more tea? The short answer is yes. But there are dangers. All teas contain chemicals that can cause kidney stones. To prevent these, take some form of calcium [kal'•see•um] with your tea.

17   Tea also contains caffeine [ka•feen']. Caffeine is the chemical in coffee that keeps some people awake at night. The amount of caffeine in a cup of tea is tiny. It would never keep you awake. So, if you want to stay awake, drink coffee. If you want to stay healthy, drink tea.

Questions

1. When did people first drink tea? Where?

2. What role did tea play in American history?

3. What are the three ways to prepare tea leaves?

4. What are the dangers of drinking tea?

Identifying Style Techniques/Applying Passage Elements

1. Find two places where the author uses humor in the article. Why do you think the author did that?

2. Why does the author call green tea a "hot" item? How does the author support that description?

3. How did the Boston Tea Party change Americans' tea drinking habits?

4. Why might modern scientists try to change American's tea drinking habits again?

Answer Key

Long Live Verdi!

Page 10: Questions
1. Barezzi paid for Verdi's studies in Milan.
2. He was grieving over the deaths of his wife and two children.
3. The opera *Nabucco* was Verdi's first big hit.
4. It was hard for Verdi to retire because he enjoyed writing music and being famous.
5. Verdi's operas are still popular because they have exciting stories, music with strong emotions, and are great shows to watch.

Page 10: Antonym/Synonym Search
1. Possible answers: liked–enjoyed; offered–afforded; ill–sick; famous–well-known; quickly–promptly; beautiful–lovely
2. Answers will vary.
3. Possible answers: poor–rich; young–old; daughter–son; bigger–smaller; good–bad; success–failure; short–tall; best–worst
4. Answers will vary.

Dogs Who "Think"

Page 16: Questions
1. They are the right size and are easy to train.
2. Poor choices for police and guide dogs are the dachshund and the poodle.
3. Guide dogs live with a family for a year whereas police dogs train in police barracks.
4. The two jobs a police dog may be given are to search for things and to break up fights.
5. About one out of every ten blind persons can learn to use a guide dog.

Page 16: Using Context Clues
1. Paragraph 8: Police dogs train in a police barracks. You are least likely to ski in a barracks.
2. Paragraph 6: But poodles don't have good judgment. Answers will vary.
3. Paragraph 9: When training starts, a police dog learns how to attack, but only does so on command. Attack on command means that the police dog will attack a person only when it is told to do so.

Dark Days

Page 21: Questions

1. Scandinavia is made up of Denmark, Finland, Iceland, Norway, and Sweden.
2. The three kinds of winter in the Arctic Circle are autumn-winter, high-winter, and spring-winter.
3. They make their own light by using bright lights in their towns.
4. The Arctic Circle is called "the land of the midnight sun" because by July, the days are so long there isn't any darkness at all.
5. Basketball would be more popular because the surrounding rivers, ponds, or lakes are usually frozen so sailing wouldn't be possible.

Page 21: Spelling Word Alert

1. Paragraph 2: The *sun* is what makes daylight. *son*
Paragraph 9: There are a *great* number of winter problems to deal with. *grate*
Paragraph 7: *There* are plays and music to enjoy. *their*
Paragraph 2: *So,* there is no daylight. *sew*
Paragraph 4: This is *seen* in many of the folktales of the land. *scene*
Paragraph 6: Bits of the sun *break* off and pass through the sky as red, blue, and white arcs of light. *brake*
Paragraph 13: On January 21, the sun rises high enough to give *four* minutes of daylight. *for*
2. *darkness;* possible sentences:
Paragraph 5: Yet everyone knows the *darkness* is on its way.
Paragraph 9: For many people, the "winter blues" come with the *darkness.*
3. Paragraph 3: There is also a great deal of snow and ice to deal with—and to *enjoy.*
Paragraph 10: To keep out the cold, walls are very *thick.*
Answers will vary.

Diamonds: Stars from Earth

Page 26: Questions

1. Answers will vary.
2. Diamonds are so rare because they need much time to form, and they are difficult to mine.
3. The two uses for diamonds are as drill points and as jewelry.
4. It has a curse on it.

Page 26: Recalling Details

1. Diamonds are made of pure carbon.
2. The four C's are cut, color, clarity, and carat weight.
3. Red is the rarest color of diamond.

4. There are about 142 carats in one ounce.

The Courage of Harry Wu

Page 32: Questions
1. Harry Wu was arrested in 1960 because he spoke out against the communists.
2. Answers will vary.
3. Wu went back to China to prove that what he was writing was true.
4. Wu was held in a tiny cell and questioned by prison guards day and night.
5. Wu was an American citizen and too many people knew and cared about him.

Page 32: Identifying Sequence
1. Wu became an American citizen before he made his fourth trip to China.
2. Correct sequence: 1. Harry Wu got a job as a geology teacher. 2. Harry Wu wrote about the prison camps. 3. Harry Wu was convicted of spying.

The Great Seal of the United States

Page 36: Questions
1. The United States decided to make a seal in 1776.
2. The Great Seal was designed by Charles Thomson and William Barton.

3. Answers will vary.
4. The color red stands for courage, the color white stands for purity, and the color blue stands for justice.

Page 36: Recognizing Stated Concepts
1. The arrows symbolize war and the olive branch peace.
2. The stripes and the ribbon in the eagle's beak both stand for unity.
3. People use eagles for symbols because they think eagles look strong and brave.
4. Franklin felt that the turkey was a more respectable bird because it was a true native of North America.

The Chunnel Under the Sea

Page 42: Questions
1. England is part of Europe through history, music, art, and trade.
2. People feared that by building a tunnel, armies might use the tunnel to invade or that a tunnel would help spread disease.
3. Answers will vary.
4. Answers will vary.
5. Travel by the Chunnel is better than travel by air because there are no flight delays, you can drive onto a

train and be across the channel in 35 minutes, or you can ride the train and be in downtown Paris in three hours.

Page 43: Using Graphs and Maps
1. Answers will vary.
2. b. how the total cost of the project was split up
3-4 Answers will vary.

Do You Have the Time?

Page 48: Questions
1. The first invention for telling time was the sundial.
2. The earth is tilted because of the change in seasons so the sun's position in the sky will be different. As a result, a sundial that is accurate in the summer is not as accurate in the winter.
3. The mechanical clock was invented about A.D. 1300.
4. Answers will vary.

Page 49: Using Forms and Schedules
1-3 Answers will vary.

The History of Money

Page 55: Questions
1. Answers will vary.
2. Cows were the standard item used as an early form of money.
3. Coins came into use about 900 B.C.

4. China made the first paper money.
5. King Henry VIII of England had this nickname. He had his own picture on the coins that were copper coated with silver; however, the silver rubbed off and made his nose look red.

Page 56: Understanding Consumer Materials
1-3 Answers will vary.

Coretta Scott King: The Dream Lives On

Page 62: Questions
1. Coretta moved to Boston to study music.
2. They shared dreams of helping African Americans win equal rights and ending the suffering that came from racial prejudice.
3. Answers will vary.

Page 62: Analyzing Characters/Identifying Main Idea
1. Answers will vary.
2. Her bravery, strength, grace, and honor are a few of the character traits that helped Coretta Scott King to continue her work after her husband's death.
3. A heading over each part is provided to point out the main idea.
4. Coretta Scott King has worked hard all of her life.

What We Know About Memory

Page 67: Questions

1. Scientists think the brain stores memory as part of a pattern.

2. The five types of memory are: 1. remembering all the words you know;
2. remembering physical skills;
3. remembering facts;
4. remembering things on a short-term basis;
5. remembering things from the recent past

3. Answers will vary.

Page 67: Comparing and Contrasting/Drawing Conclusions

1. Events from the recent past is the type of memory that fades the most over time.

2. Riding a bicycle uses a memory involving remembering a physical skill. This type of memory is different in that it is a repeated skill used many times over the years whereas short-term memory lasts only a few seconds.

3. Prior knowledge of a subject helps you remember new facts by connecting them with old facts to make stronger memories.

4. Learning a new language helps improve your memory by exercising your brain.

Black Soldiers: Unsung Heroes

Page 72: Questions

1. Blacks helped the Union cause early in the war by building roads and forts and by carrying supplies to the front lines.

2. The Emancipation Proclamation changed the purpose of the war by including the fight to end slavery altogether.

3. A black regiment attacked the fort.

4. Nearly 200,000 blacks fought for the Union during the Civil War and about 37,638 died.

Page 72: Identifying Cause and Effect/Summarizing and Paraphrasing/Finding Supporting Evidence

1. They didn't think they would need them.

2. Blacks were finally allowed to fight because the war was going badly for the North.

3–4 Answers will vary.

A Walk Through the Rain Forest

Page 77: Questions

1. Answers will vary.

2. Bamboo is the fastest growing rain forest plant.

3. The plants take in the nutrients from the food in the soil so quickly that the

soil doesn't have a chance to build up.
4. Many rain forests are destroyed because farmers in these areas need the land to grow crops.
5. The soil is very thin and washes away easily thus causing flooding.

Page 77: Predicting Outcomes/Identifying Fact and Opinion
1–3 Answers will vary.

How to Survive Anything

Page 84: Questions
1. Answers will vary.
2. If you can't fight off a strong dog, curl up into a ball with your hands over your head.
3. You shouldn't eat greasy foods or drink alcohol before you board a boat.
4. You should soak towels in water to place over your mouth and nose to help filter out the smoke in a room or building that is on fire.
5. You should swerve to the right to avoid a head-on car crash.

Page 84: Recognizing Author's Purpose/Making Generalizations
1. The author's purpose for writing this article is to explain ways to survive dangerous situations.
2-3 Answers will vary.

Tea: To Your Health

Page 89: Questions
1. People first drank tea about 5000 years ago in China.
2. Tea played a role in American history as part of the Boston Tea Party.
3. The three ways to prepare tea leaves are by steaming, drying, or fermenting the leaves.
4. The dangers are developing kidney stones and feeling the effects from the caffeine in a cup of tea.

Page 89: Identifying Style Techniques/Applying Passage Elements
1. Answers will vary.
2. The author calls green tea a "hot" item because there are some exciting things being discovered about it. Answers will vary.
3. Many of them became coffee drinkers.
4. Answers will vary.